"Kids Say the Darndest Things to Santa Claus"

25 Year of Santa Stories - A Special Forward

For the past 25 years, I've volunteered as Santa Claus for organizations that did not have the funds to hire a Santa. This included places like boys & girls clubs, children's hospitals, military bases, women's & children's shelters, fire victim shelters, schools, churches, community centers, temporary housing centers, casinos, apartments, and everything in between. I got my start portraying Santa when a good friend of mine became ill the night before a large boys & girls club appearance and suggested I fill in for him. I did, and the rest is history and now immortalized in text.

I have to do a special shout out to all of the wonderful, amazing, and selfless elves at all of the locations who give their time and talents to help make memories for kids every Holiday season. I have always enjoyed watching their reactions: the unfiltered, honest, humorous, and heartfelt comments of the "little characters" we encounter. There's something about being at a Santa appearance for several hours that is very different than that of a shopping mall. Malls typically feature a quick hello, what's your name & age, what is your wish for Christmas, smile for the photo, and done. Other than on TV, books, videos, etc. kids today don't get to spend any real quality time with jolly old Saint Nick. At Santa appearances for organizations, many run 2- 4 hours which gives kids who may be too timid initially to meet Santa the time to observe things and finally build up the courage to get their "Santa legs." One of the most important things I explain to parents and grandparents is to not force kids to meet Santa. Since there is often several hours for the event, I encourage them to let the kids warm up to the idea rather than push them into it. Imagine a kid, especially a first timer, looking at this icon with a long white beard, full plush red suit, and the ability to grant presents and miracles. Why would they just immediately go up and meet him, especially after their parents and grandparents have told them constantly "not to speak to strangers!" All in good time is my motto to the kids.

I'm often asked what's the most amazing place I've been Santa at. There are myriad mesmerizing situations; however, the one that always shines out is the Pueblo of Acoma in New Mexico at their ancestral site, "The Rock," located on a 365+ foot mesa. Acoma "Sky City" is the oldest inhabited community in North America. Several hundred children gathered for Christmas Day services at their 16th century Mission. I arrived on the back of the Pueblo's fire truck (with the EMT unit following). There in the Spanish Mission, I presented blankets to the Matriarchs of the 13 clans, presented a plate of food at the altar, and caught my Santa sleeve on the hand of the hand-carved wooden Christ child which had been presented to the Pueblo by the King of Spain (which in itself is a whole other story). I presented plates of fruits and nuts to the Pueblo Elders and War Chiefs around a traditional bonfire. Later I visited and gave presents to 200 children of the Pueblo's families. When we got back to the volunteer Fire Station, one of the firefighters asked me "how do you do that?" I told him I never really thought about it; I just do it. It was a long, meaningful, and magical day. Several months later, I received a Special Commendation from the

Pueblo Governor to: Don Kennedy (Santa Claus). It meant a great deal to me.

Another question I constantly get is how Santa doesn't cry or laugh at the amazing comments and stories kids share. It's important that Santa remains an anonymous, independent, non-judgmental sounding board for kids so that they feel safe, secure, and open to sharing. My secret, which I've shared with the elves, is to bite the inside of my cheek if it gets really hard to contain my reaction. Yes, I've gone home numerous nights like I had just left the dentist! I also tell elves to just turn away and let their emotions out which, of course, doesn't work for Santa directly facing a child.

How many Santa suits does St. Nick go through in a season? Yes, accidents do happen and Santa does need to be prepared. I always keep a second suit with me for just these occasions. A typical Holiday Season is 3 or 4 suits.

How many times does Santa get his beard pulled? I have stopped counting!

A question that often comes up is what to do if a child says something that may indicate problems or issues at home. This has happened a dozen or so times over the years. I was trained to share this with the organizers of the appearance who can then follow up with the correct authorities who deal with these situations.

Another question often asked is for my favorite humorous and heartwarming stories. Hence, this collection of 25 years of Santa stories. Each year I have kept a log of stories jotted down in the car right after an appearance while the memory is fresh. The past 4 years, I prepared a Top 10 list of the funniest and most heartfelt stories and shared them on Facebook with my family and friends. This collection of the Top 100 is the result of so many folks saying "you really need to write a book."

So, this is for every child, sibling, aunt, uncle, parent, grandparent, family friend, relative, elf, Santa appearance organizers, and Santa's everywhere.

Santa Stories – The Very First Time

25 years ago, in early December, a close friend of mine shared with me that he was a volunteer Santa. He made appearances at various holiday parties for organizations that did not have the funds to rent a Santa. He suggested for some time that I should dress up as an Elf and join him. The night before a Boys & Girls Club children's party, he came down with a virus. He suggested that I go in his place. I had a hundred questions but nevertheless agreed, taking his Santa suit and nervously practicing my "ho ho ho" in the car ride over.

100 children from the ages 4–8 were waiting at the center draped with festive holiday décor. A dozen staff volunteers and several dozen parents were present as well. There were

refreshments and small gifts for all the kids.

Santa had a Head Elf and 2 Santa's helpers. Sitting on a large stuffed chair, the children all sang holiday songs. Then the announcement was made to line up single-file and approach Santa. The Head Elf introduced each child to Santa by their first name. I then asked each child their age and had them hold up their fingers to show their age, something I still practice to this day. Santa matched each finger with theirs, which created a special type of high five.

Santa then asked each child what their wishes were for Christmas, followed by a photo and giving the kids a large candy cane. So far, so good. I remember thinking that this isn't too hard.

The next child came up, a 6-year-old boy, who replied when I asked what his wishes were, "Well, I wrote you a letter, don't you remember?" Thinking fast, I told him that Mrs. Claus took care of all of the letters. OK, that worked.

A dozen kids later and I had my first "accident" when a very excited little boy "urped" on Santa's leg. This was when I realized that Santa needs a backup suit at all appearances. The best I could do in this case was take a short break, clean up as best as I can, and go back at it.

A few kids later, a little girl came up, stared at Santa and blurted out, "You better drink skim milk or 2% milk cause you look really fat!" Her mother was horrified but I told her that Mrs. Claus had me on a new diet. She seemed satisfied with that. Being puked on aside, this was becoming heartwarmingly fun.

Donning the Santa suit taught me several things but mainly that you need to be quick on your feet and ready for just about anything. You need to listen carefully and not promise the world. I was also in total wonder at these amazing little characters, how their minds worked, and what they had to say.

On went the night, about 2 ½ hours in all. I changed, went out to the car, and wrote down about a dozen notes of what the kids had said. On the drive home, I realized that this was one of the most meaningful days of my life. The next day, I returned the Santa suit to my friend (washed) and told him about my experience. He was most happy that his prediction that I would be a good Santa was correct. And, as they say, the rest is history!

Chapter 1 – Military

Military bases and National Guard visits by Santa are extraordinary because in many cases the children have parents who are deployed. Between the kids and the spouses, Santa needs special answers to questions about their loved ones. I have had countless encounters where it was up to Santa to keep their hope alive, and I've also been blessed with reacquainting loved ones on the spot. There is nothing like either feeling, what a blessing to be a part of it. Children who have parents that are deployed often have bottled up emotions that seem to flow when talking with Santa. They'll say things like, "I don't want mommy to feel bad so I don't say anything about missing my daddy," and then it all comes out. Service to one's state and country is very special to begin with, but selflessly leaving one's family for long periods of time is even more special.

Santa has to provide hope, encouragement, comfort, and good cheer for these special families in need.

At a military base children's party, a 7-year-old boy was introduced to Santa by the Head Elf as Kyle from Kailua, whose daddy was stationed here and was currently deployed. His mom was also working. Santa displayed the "Shaka" sign and said, "Aloha, Kyle from Kailua, Mele Kalikimaka!" Kyle's eyes lit up and his jaw dropped. He stared at Santa Claus for 10 seconds before finally saying, "OMG! OMG! OMG!" He leaned in and gave Santa a big bear hug. Santa told Kyle he knew exactly where Kailua was (Oahu, Hawaii) and that he loved to fly his sleigh to all of the islands. Kyle sat on the stage near Santa for another hour, then displayed the "Shaka" sign, smiled a big, wide smile, and waved goodbye to Santa. Santa returned the "Shaka" sign and again said "Mele Kalikimaka! (Merry Christmas)" as the boy walked away. Later the Elf told Santa that Kyle had seemed so sad when he first came into the Recreation Center.

A family of 4 came to meet Santa at the children's party. Mom and the 3 kids, ages 5, 7, and 8, stood in line and finally made it to Santa. The oldest child said, "We're all here except daddy but it's okay, maybe next year. Please don't be mad at us cause he's not here, we all misses him so much." Mom had secretly arranged a Facetime call and let Santa in on the plan. All of the sudden, daddy was on the live call and we all joined in. Big smiles all around the globe.

A 7-year-old boy came up to Santa by himself and said, "My daddy told me that if I wasn't a better boy in the next couple weeks before Christmas, I was gonna just get coal in my stocking on the fireplace." The little guy looked very puzzled and asked Santa, "What's coal?"

A 7-year-old girl came to see Santa and said, "My dad's an air traffic 'troller and he said he's cleared the skies for you Christmas Eve cause we don't needs no issues up there with the sleigh and all the toys on it."

A 6-year-old girl handed Santa a note with some numbers on it. She said, "That's our 'curity code cause we gots no fireplace and I don't wants yous to get locked out!" After she was done, Santa handed the note to her dad and suggested he may want to get it changed since "you don't know how many other Santas she may have given it out to." The dad replied, "Thanks, she's been very worried for weeks now since she saw Santa on TV going down a chimney with a big bag of toys and our house doesn't have one."

A little girl, age 6, came up and said, "Mommies in Ganistan and I misses her so when yous goes there can yous finds her and tell her I loves her, put her in the sleigh, and brings her back to me?" Her dad was standing nearby and didn't know what to say. Santa smiled at her and said, "Your mommy can't come back right away but Santa knows exactly where she is and when I fly there, I'll stop and give her a big hug from you and ask her to come home real soon, OK?" The little girl said, "OK, thanks yous." Dad was relieved plus a big smile on his face as well.

At a Christmas party for Air Force adults, Santa wore a large bright button that read, "Need Jet Escort Christmas Eve!" It was the hit of the evening with everyone taking photos and selfies with Santa. As the evening ended, a dozen different airmen stopped by and said the same thing, "I'm your man Santa. Just let me know where and what time."

A 7-year-old boy at a military base party came up and told Santa that his daddy had recently gone hunting and shot a deer. The little guy wanted to make sure that it wasn't one of Santa's. "Can you go outside and make sure Rudolph is there and all the others?" he said. "We don't want it to slow you down if you don't has all of them you knows," he added as he looked over at his dad. Santa told the boy that all of the reindeer are accounted for. The boy wiped his brow and said, "OK, cool, cause we can't have no problems you knows." His dad smiled at Santa and gave him the thumbs up.

A young boy and girl came up to Santa with their mom at a base recreation center and handed Santa a letter. They asked Santa if he could deliver it to their daddy in Heaven when he was flying by. Mom explained that her husband had passed recently due to combat injuries. The kids said they wanted their daddy to know that they loved him. The little girl added, "It's OK if Jesus wants to read it too."

An 8-year-old girl came up and said, "I been standing in line a long time and I think this whole thing is not very efficient." Mom was standing near and had a horrified look on her face. The girl added, "Maybe you need to go all online and streamline the process." Continuing, she said, "I'll put a proposal together for you and email it to you, OK. You do have email, right?" Mom told her daughter that it was time to go and let the other children visit with Santa. This time, Santa was the one with the relieved look on his face.

A family of 3 children, ages 4, 6, and 8, came with mom to see Santa at a base children's party. Their dad had been on a mission but had returned home recently and kept it a secret, staying with friends. Only Santa and his Head Elf knew what was about to happen. The oldest girl spoke for the family and said, "Our daddy's in 'RACK and we misses him and mommy misses him too. We all talked and if you don't give us no presents, would you have room in the sleigh on Christmas Eve to stop in 'RACK and bring him home to us?" Santa happily replied, "You don't need to wait until Christmas Eve. Santa stopped in 'RACK tonight on the way to the party and had lots of room in the sleigh." Pointing to the recreation center door, the serviceman walked through with the Head Elf. All 3 of the kids' eyes balooned, their jaws dropped, and they nearly knocked their dad over.

Mom almost passed out. Santa went back to the line of children. About a half hour later, the 6-year-old boy came back in the line and said, "Now that daddy's home, could we maybes gets a couple presents Christmas Eve, please Santa?"

Chapter 2 – Fire Shelters

Fire shelters, temporary housing centers, school gyms, church halls... wherever families gather to take refuge after a horrific fire sweeps through their community, Santa visits provide a different type of challenge. I have made dozens of visits over the years but especially to Los Angeles, Santa Barbara, and Paradise, California in recent years. Providing words of comfort, hope, encouragement, and unity are crucial at these times. Being able to give a holiday gift to a child of a displaced family can bring a wide smile and some sense of normalcy at an unsure time. I will always remember one relief worker explaining it to me this way: "the next time you drive home and turn the corner into your neighborhood, picture nothing there at all. All gone, nothing to come home to." Then comes trying to regroup, plan, and rebuild. Such courage, such sense of community, such resolve. The other aspect of this are the first responders, relief workers, support staff, and shelter employees who work with these families for days, weeks, and even months at hand. These folks also need a hug from Santa as well as the encouragement to keep giving, caring, and sharing their passion.

A family of 4 at a fire shelter had just gathered before Santa arrived. The mom told her children, ages 4, 6, and 8, that they wouldn't be able to have a Christmas this year as they had just lost everything in a fire. The youngest 2 children asked their mom why? Mom did her best to explain and finally said, "Because Santa wouldn't be able to find us now." An hour later, Santa arrived at the shelter. Coming in the room, the little boy ran and grabbed Santa around the boots and proclaimed "I knew you'd find us. I knew you'd find us." As the staff and Santa passed out gifts, mom broke down with tears of joy. She then told me how she had just talked with them about missing Christmas. Santa told her to always believe, always hope, and always celebrate whenever you could, especially having her children alive and well.

A little girl told Santa that her only wish for Christmas was to rescue her toy "Teddy" from their destroyed house, as he was "all alone." Mom and dad told Santa on the side that she hadn't slept the whole night through for a week as she was so worried. Her dad had purchased an identical bear that day and gave it to Santa to present to their daughter. Santa told the little girl that the Elves had gone to their home to get "Teddy". The girl grabbed the bear and almost hugged the stuffing right out of him.

4 children and their mom had lost their apartment in a fire just a few days earlier. The oldest girl, 8, said the kids had all gotten together and didn't want gifts if Santa could give their mom a big hug. "Mommy is so sad, so could you just make her smile again and be happy?" the girl asked. Santa said he would. The kids all smiled and the girl added, "We'll write a letter to Mrs. Claus so she doesn't get jealous, OK?"

A little girl, 4 or 5, told Santa, "We gots no cookies cause it's all burnded up. Is that OK, so you won't be mad at us?" Santa replied that "it's OK, I'll just take double cookies next year when you get a new home." The little girl smiled and said, Sweet!"

A 7-year-old boy asked Santa if it was "OK if I rides with you in the sleigh cause I gots nowhere to live now." Santa told the little guy that his mommy and daddy were getting him a new home to live in. The boy replied, "Oh, OK, but a ride in the sleigh would be really cool!"

A boy, 6, told Santa that he "losted all of my toys in a fire but mostly I miss Rover." Rover was his puppy, his first and only pet. His Uncle had arranged to bring a similar puppy to the shelter. Santa told the little guy, "Well, I stopped at your house and found this little puppy," and reached into his toy sack and pulled him out. The boy got the biggest smile on his face and hugged his new Rover and cried tears of joy. His Uncle looked at Santa and said, "This is what Christmas is all about, isn't it?" Santa smiled and replied, "Yes, you did a good thing here. you're a wonderful Uncle." It's the little things that can truly make a difference.

A 7-year-old girl told Santa, "We got no house now so it's OK if we don't gets no toys cause we don't gots nowhere to put them." Santa told the girl that she would be getting a new place to live real soon. The girl smiled and said, "Oh, really, can you just do layaway then for me?"

At a fire shelter, 3 kids, ages 4-6, looked very sad. The oldest girl told Santa, "We gots no oven to bakes you cookies and no milk. Will you still likes us?" Santa smiled, huddled them together and said, "Not only do I like you but I love you and always will, cookies or no cookies." The little boy grabbed Santa and shouted, "I tolds them! I tolds them!"

Chapter 3 – Shelters

Shelters for women and children who are seeking safety, relief, and temporary housing are a true challenge for Santa. Due to the need for security and safety, Santa is taken to the shelters by staff without knowing the location until arrival. The staff brief Santa on each of the situations one by one so that he is aware of any special needs. I have seen enough black eyes, split lips, broken bones, and cigarette burns to last a lifetime, but I also know that this is where Santa needs to be more than perhaps any other situation. Providing a hug, a kind word, a big smile, a gift, a treat, and hope is key. The staff themselves also need the same type of thank you and encouragement for their tremendous efforts in helping keep families together, safe, and secure. I often say at the end of the Holiday season that I have gained much more than I have given. Shelters are the biggest part of that feeling.

A 6-year-old boy at a shelter met Santa, smiled and said, "It's been a rough couple week so I'll takes just bout anythings you gots in your bag Santa!"

3 children ranging in ages from 4 to 7 came up to Santa and said, "We don't needs nothing only if you can help mommy stop crying cause she's been real sad. We promise to be real good too Santa. We promises."

A 6-year-old boy told Santa, "Can you tells everybodys to love us kids and not hurt us please?" If that doesn't tug on the heart strings, nothing will.

A little girl, 6, took Santa by the hand and walked him to the window. She looked out, got a tear in her eye and said, "All I wants for Christmas is to goes outside and play with all of my friends like I's used to." Santa told her that soon it will all be better and she can play with her friends again. She looked up at Santa and said, "Promise?" Santa smiled and said, "You bet, sweetheart!" The little girl gave him a big hug. Her mom came up just then and the girl looked at her and said, "Santa said it's gonna be OKs." Mom gave Santa a big hug and said, "Thank you so much. She really needed that, and honestly, so did I."

A family of 4 children came up to Santa, and the oldest said to him, "Santa can you please dance with our mommy so she can smile again, please?" Santa said sure and asked their mom to dance. They danced for about 5 minutes with the kids standing near. Mom was kind of surprised about the whole gesture and asked Santa what was going on. Santa told her of her children's request. She smiled, teared up, and told Santa it was their favorite thing to do together whenever it rained outside: putting on music and dancing all over their house. She told Santa, "Leave it to a child to focus on that fun time when things are so rough right now for all of us." Santa reassured her and said that her children would help her get through it all.

Chapter 4 – Children's Center Parties

Boys & Girls Clubs, Community Children's Centers, schools, and churches are a huge part of the season. Visiting with several hundred of children at each of these sites is such fun! Every time I think I've seen and heard it all, something new comes up. There is something intangible about the Holiday season that is simply magical. Often kids come dressed in their best party clothes for the event. One of my favorite things is doing repeat yearly appearances at the same event and watching the children grow up. Another favorite is watching older kids introduce their younger sisters and brothers to Santa and showing them how to be part of the whole experience. Being visited by entire families is also a real joy with all the children, parents, grandparents, relatives, and friends joining in. One amazing blessing which never changes for me is being a child's first Santa. Imagine the feeling of holding a weeks or months old child for their first photo with Santa. I have been so very fortunate over these many years.

A boy, 7, came up to Santa and said, "I's figures that there's lots a left-over candy and cookies and gifts and stuff when there's no oneses home on Christmas Eve, so I's willing to take all that stuff off your hands, just saying."

A boy, 6, came up with his mom and had an orange circle all the way around his mouth. His mom said, "Tell Santa why you have orange color all around your mouth." He looked up and said, "Cause I was eating pisgetti!" "Spaghetti," she corrected him. "And someone was in too big of a hurry to get here so he didn't wash up," she continued. Santa smiled and said, "I like pisgetti too." The little guy got all excited and said, "See, Santa 'nounces it like me too." His mom corrected him again, "Pronounces." The little boy leaned in close to Santa's ear and said, "I just can't win with her."

An 8-year-old boy at a Boys & Girls Club party told Santa, "I put our cell phone number on my letter to you just in case you get lost." He continued, "You do have that GGGPPSS on your sleigh, right?"

A 7-year-old boy said, "So, is there really a big pole there where you live cause that's what it's called?" He added "Oh, and if you need help eating all of the cookies that you get, then I'm your man, OK!"

Two 7-year-old girls at a children's center came up to the stage excitedly and blurted out, "So, Santa, guess what it's called when one of your Elves takes a selfie?" They continued,

"It's an Elfie, get it, cause it's a selfie and an Elf, that's why."

A 7-year-old boy at a Boys & Girls Club asked Santa, "How does the whole sleigh thing work flying, cause I don't sees no engine?" Santa replied that it was Christmas magic, just like how the reindeer fly. The boy replied, "OK, cool, cause that was gonna be my next question. Mom and dad says I ask too many questions like where babies come from and stuff like that." Santa told him that babies were also a miracle. He looked at Santa and said, "My sister ain't no miracle Santa. She's a real pain!"

A 7-year-old girl from a third world country came up to Santa and said, "I don't need anything for Christmas this year, but can you bring stuff to where I used to live cause lots of kids don't have any shoes to wear?"

A little girl, 6, came up to Santa with a big red and green sugar cookie and said, "Here, you can start early!"

A family of 4 little boys came up all decked out in matching black pants, white shirts, and red bow ties. Mom, dad, and the grandparents were all there. After telling their Christmas wishes, it was photo time. Trying to get all 4 to look at the camera and smile at the same time was quite a project. Finally, it was all over and the oldest boy looked at Santa, pointed to his bow tie and asked, "Can I gets rid of this now, please?" Santa pointed to mom and said, "It's your parent's decision." The boy replied, "I guess I'm stuck with it all night. I tried!"

A girl, 7, came up to Santa and asked, "When you go everywhere, can you ask people not to kill each other cause that's all I see on TV?"

She added, "Can you just tell them to be nice to each other, please?"

A little boy named Alexander proudly marched up the steps at a children's center party and announced, "Last year I didn't want my picture took, but now I'm a big boy. I'm 5, so let's do this!"

A girl, 8, asked Santa very sadly if he could help "Nana remember things cause sometimes she forgets my name." Santa said that "Even if that happens, her Nana would always love her just the same." The little girl smiled and replied, "Oh, I get it. It's OK then, thanks". She ran off and Santa saw her later in the party walking and holding hands with her mom and Nana. All 3 were smiling, drinking hot chocolate, and laughing. Three generations all together enjoying the Holidays. It doesn't get much better than that.

A 7-year-old girl from a third world country came up and told Santa, "I don't needs nothing but can you bring some food to my country where I used to live, because lots and lots of kids there are starving?"

A very stoic little boy, 6, from an Eastern European country, was standing back from the stage at a children's center party. His father kept pushing him forward, but the little guy just wasn't ready to meet Santa yet. I often tell parents not to push kids into visiting with Santa; just give them time. About an hour went by of him coming up to the stage, pausing, going back and coming forward again. Finally, the big moment came and he climbed up the stairs and stood before Santa. He had a toy Transformer with him, and he handed it to Santa. Santa smiled and said that the toy was his to keep as a Christmas present. The little boy almost smiled and replied, "Cool!"

Then he stepped down off the stage and ran off to play. Several more times during the evening, he came back to the stage, almost smiled again, and waved at Santa. The ice was broken.

A girl, 7, came up to Santa and had a very serious look on her face. She said, "I gots a real problem." Santa asked the girl what was wrong. She replied, "Well, do you need gluten-free cookies cause Nana's on a cruise and I dont's know how to take the gluten out?"

A little boy, 6, came up to the stage with his mom and waited his turn to see Santa. When he reached Santa, he pulled out a large piece of paper. His mom looked at Santa and said, "Oh, oh, I hope you're ready for this. He has a very curious mind, Santa!" The boy looked at his mom and back at Santa. He said, "Let's gets us started here, OK." He held up the paper and started right in: "So, where does the poop go from the reindeer when they're flying up there, and why are elves short and hows do you goes down the chimney and not get all black and…." At this point, his mom stopped him and said, "Honey, those are all very good questions but Santa's got lots of other children to see him, so how about you just tell him what you'd like for Christmas now." The boy put his paper away and pulled out another piece of paper and started reading a long list of Christmas wishes that included a pony, a pet dog, a video game, a toy car, a tree house, and so forth. His mom stopped him again and told Santa, "Maybe we should just go back to the questions!"

A girl, 6, finished up telling Santa her list of Christmas wishes. As she turned to leave, Santa coughed from being sick, an unfortunate trend that comes from meeting so many boys and girls. The little girl turned back around, put her hands on her hips and said, "You better takes your Flintstones vitamins, cause we's don't needs no sick Santa, you knows!"

A little boy, 5, came up the stairs with his eyes real big and his jaw dropped and blurted out. "OMG! You are real likes the M & M's say on TV!"

A brother and sister came up to see Santa and the girl said, "We just moved and our new house doesn't have a fireplace and a chimney." The boy chimed in, "So how is this going to work now cause this could be a major problem, you know?"

A girl, 8, came to see Santa with a very serious look on her face. She said, "You really do need to get a Santa App. Nobody writes letters anymore!"

Chapter 5 – Young Love

Young love is one of the most precious things Santa gets to observe. Two kids holding hands, visiting with Santa, and telling him their hopes and dreams is something to behold. These very special couples are often hilarious especially when they are very, very serious. It goes back to Santa never showing too much emotion in some situations because you never know the full story when they stop by. Kids pick up so much from television, videos, the internet, and other sources that they are often way ahead of Santa! I have lost track of how many times I've been asked by kids to marry them and pronounce them man and wife.

At a military base children's party, a boy and a girl (both 6 and holding hands) came up to Santa Claus. The boy asked Santa if "You cans marriage us before our mommies come back?" The little girl looked directly at Santa, stood very straight and tall and said, "I do!" Just then, the 2 moms arrived bringing hot chocolate. The 2 kids raised their arms in the air, shouted "too late" and ran off. The moms told Santa that the kids lived a block apart and had been "a couple" for about 6 months.

A 7-year-old boy at a children's center party had already gone through the line and had his photo taken. He came back up to Santa and asked, "Can I talks to you?" Santa told him, "Sure, just come back when the line is gone." The boy waited patiently, came back up and asked, "Can I talks to you now?" Santa again said, "Sure. What's on your mind, young man?" The boy blurted out, "I needs to go with you when you leave tonight for the pole cause this girl in my class, Sarah, keeps trying to kiss me. I needs to be in witness tection!" Santa said that sounded very, very serious. The boy replied, "Yes, she keeps trying to kiss me. Please, can I goes with you in the sleigh?" Santa asked if Sarah was pretty and the little guy replied, "NO!!!" Santa told the boy that when he got older, he'd probably like girls to kiss him. "NEVER," the boy sternly replied. Running out of answers, Santa asked the boy if he thought his family would miss him. The boy looked at the ground and thought for a while before finally saying, "I knows but I really needs to be in witness tection." He continued, "Please, can I goes with you? I'll be real good in the sleigh, I promises." Santa replied that the sleigh was already full tonight. The boy replied, "Well, it was worth a try."

Santa was leaving a shelter to ride to another when a 7-year-old boy spotted him on the same block. The boy came running, leaving his parents to try to catch up. The boy yelled out, "OMG Santa, I wrotes you a letter and now I gotta change my wish cause I gotta 'prose to Amber on Christmas Day so Jason doesn't get her cause she's a hottie." Before Santa could speak, the boy continued, "So does you goes by Jared's on the way to my house, so you could stop and get a ring? I gots lots of rope so we can tie knots and stuff. I gotta does all of this by June cause that's when peoples marrys, you knows?" By this moment, his parents had made it all the way down the street and were listening intently. Santa finally had a chance to get a word in. He asked the boy if it wasn't better to wait awhile till he was older. His parents smiled. The boy replied, "Oh, till I'm 8? Oh, ok, then let's stick with the XBox."

Chapter 6 – Siblings

Sibling rivalries are such a fun part of Santa's visits. Typically, it's a boy and girl, although some situations involve families with multiple brothers and sisters. Telling on each other, of course, is the number one situation that comes up. Often the brother and sister are separated in the line to see Santa. As each one comes up and starts talking, Santa can almost pick out the person they are referring to. These are often the absolute funniest of all Santa visits with kids. At the same time, the kid telling on the other sibling is often very serious, so it's important for Santa to try to keep a straight face and listen very intently.

At a children's center, a 7-year-old boy leaned in close to Santa's ear and said, "My sister wrote you a Christmas letter so I needed to check and see if she ratted me out." Santa got a real chuckle out of that one.

A girl, 8, came up to Santa at a military base party and said, "My brother is so totally out of control that I need you to put him in your sleigh and dump him off on Mars!"

At a Boys & Girls Club party, an 8-year-old girl came up and said, "Have I got something to tell you Santa Claus!" She continued, "My little brother ate your whole plate of cookies so Nana had to bake a whole new tray just for you." She put her hands on her hips and said, "My work is done here," and marched off triumphantly. About an hour later, a little guy came up and said, "I's gots in trouble cause I was hungry and ates your cookies, so I bets yous gonna hear 'bout it. I'm sorry."

An 8-year-old boy at a military base children's party came up to Santa and announced, "I don't need a toy this year, but I need your help instead." He asked Santa if when he came to his house on Christmas Eve, Santa could "take my sister in your sleigh and drop her off far, far away in some other Galaxy like on Star Wars, cause she's gotta go, Santa!"

A little boy, 6, introduced to Santa by the Head Elf as Jacob replied, "I's not Jacob. I's Jake." He talked a bit with Santa, gave his Christmas wish list, and had his photo taken. Then he leaned in close to Santa's ear and said, "Can I's talks to you in private?" Santa told the boy "Sure." He leaned back in close again and said, "My sister blames me for all kinds of stuff I ain't done, so if my record looks real bad, it ain't all my fault."

2 children from the same family came up to Santa together: a 7-year-old boy and an 8-year-old girl. The boy went first and said he had been "really, really, really, really, really

good this past year." His sister gave him the tilted head look. The boy changed his story to just "really, really good." She rolled her eyes and looked at him and said, "Oh, really?" He got all his courage up and replied, "That's my's story and I's stickin to it!"

A very serious 7-year-old girl came up to Santa Claus, put her hands on her hips and said, "My brother is just out of control now, and something must be done about it!"

A 5-year-old boy at an employee's children's party came to Santa and said, "My sister wrotes you our Christmas letter cause she's bossy and takes over everythings, and I'll bets she didn't asked for nothing for me neither."

Chapter 7 – Hospitals

Going to a medical facility to visit children who are ill is a real challenge for Santa. Similar to shelters though, it is a place with great need. Often children's wings at hospitals will put together a party to make things a bit brighter especially right before Christmas. Kids who have to spend Christmas Eve and Christmas Day are especially vulnerable to sadness, so it's an important two days for Santa to be out and about. Veterans medical facilities also hold kids' parties which are often for grandchildren as well. Hospice is also a very special place for a last Christmas Santa visit. The wonderful caregivers, EMTS, and all medical staff are such blessings to ill kids and adults alike. One RN told me years ago that they try not to get too close to patients because of the emotional toll it takes when kids get more ill or even pass away. I understand that now.

Niki, 6, was in a motor vehicle accident and had a broken arm and leg plus lots of bruises and lacerations. Her mom was in the car driving and was now in a medically-induced coma. Her dad is in the military, newly stationed in Las Vegas and now deployed. The family had just moved to the area and had no close family or friends. The hospital called and Santa Claus came to the room. Niki's dad was now in route back to Las Vegas from Germany. Santa spent time with the little girl watching movies, reading books, talking, and having Jell-O and juice. Niki dosed off several times during the evening. Her dad arrived and she smiled and said, "Look daddy, Santa's here. Can we take him home?" She continued, "We had so much fun. I don't want him to go back to the North Pole." Dad took over and Santa quietly left. Several days later, Santa received a text that read, "I got your text # from the hospital staff. THANKS for being there for our PRINCESS. No words, no way to say what we feel, no way to explain, being there all those hours, your care, your love, your words, you calmed her, you reassured her, you kept her safe, secure and calm. Thank you, Sir. RESPECT SIR! GOD SPEED SIR! From a grateful dad and the Mrs. Yes, she's much better too and both are healing well."

At a children's hospital wing, a 7-year-old boy was going to have surgery the following day. He told Santa, "So I'm not going to be home when you come for Christmas Eve, can you just give my toys to our next-door neighbors kids cause their dad lost his job and they don't have any money now?" Santa told the little guy that he would still get lots of presents. Plus, Santa talked with the boy's parents and got the address of the family in need. Santa was able to make a special stop on Christmas Eve and surprised the family's 5 kids with presents.

At a children's party at a Veterans hospital, a little 6-year-old girl came up to Santa and proclaimed, "My daddy's leg fell off, so can you and the Elves make him a new one, cause he needs to dance at my wedding, OK?"

Babies are always very special, because it's their first time being with Santa Claus. They don't know what's going on at the time, but they will in years to come seeing photos. A little girl, barely 3 months old, was with her grandmother in a children's hospital wing. Santa held her and the grandmother beamed. She said, "Our precious little one almost didn't make it, Santa. Her heart stopped 3 times during delivery." She continued, "So, I guess we already got our Christmas wish come true, right Santa?" Right indeed.

Two girls, both 7, came up to Santa and said, "We're BFF's now so can you ask Jesus to make us both well so we can go play outside together?"

A 6-year-old girl at a Veterans hospital children's party came up to Santa Claus and said, "I don't need anything, but could you come with me?" Santa said yes, and the little girl took him by the hand into a hospital room. She said, "That's my daddy's bed and next to his is another mans. My daddy said he gots no one so let's go make him happy." The girl brought Santa over to the man and she said, "Mister, I brought you Santa so you can smile." The man could barely hold his emotions together.

Boy, 7, came up to Santa and asked, "Can the Elves make me some more hair cause I lost all mine and I can't get any hotties like this you know?"

A 7-year-old girl in the hospital had broken both arms and a leg in a bicycle accident. She told Santa that she probably couldn't have Christmas this year in the hospital, because she couldn't open her presents. Santa arranged to come back on Christmas Day. Her family was there and several of the hospital staff dressed up as Elves. We held each present up to her thumb and index finger to touch, then the Elves opened each gift for her. Smiles all around.

Santa was told in advance that a little girl, age 6, might not make it to Christmas Day due to her terminal illness. It was a week before Christmas. The girl asked Santa, "If you sees Angels up in the sky when you're in your sleigh, cause I thinks I wants to be one." Santa stopped at a party store the next day and delivered a set of costume wings for her parents to give to her on Christmas Eve. Her parents texted Santa a few weeks later that she held on until the day after Christmas. They said they were both very sure she was wearing wings now.

Chapter 8 - The Naughty List

One of the great mysteries for Santa over the years is why it's only boys who are so worried about being on the Naughty List! Then again, coming from a family of 3 boys, I suppose I do understand. I can't remember the last time a little girl came up and wanted to know if they were on that particular list. Kids are always more frantic about it too the closer it gets to Christmas Eve and Christmas Day. Santa can sense the panic in the young voices. I can also tell when the parents have been using the Naughty List as a last warning for their kids. Naughty or nice is very crucial in the Holiday Season.

An 8-year-old boy at an employee's children's party was standing by the steps to the stage where Santa was sitting. He finally found the courage to come up and stood very close to

Santa's ear. He was very nervous and shifted from one leg to the other before finally saying, "I'm disclosure that I been bad most of the year, but it's really not my fault cause stuff just happens to me." Santa just smiled and the boy continued, "So, I bet I'm on the naughty list for sure." Santa told the little guy that he had all month long in December to be extra special good to help make up for it. The boy said, "Oh, yeah, I guess, but isn't there like a Pardon app I could use instead?"

Boy, 7, at a military base party asked Santa if "Bad stuffs you do rolls over or what?" Santa replied, "No, you start fresh every year." The little boy wiped his brow and said, "Cool, cause I'm probably like right on the edges, you knows?"

Another 7-year-old boy at a military base party waited by the stage until all of the other children had gone through the line. He then marched up the steps while hoisting a $5 bill. He asked Santa, "Can this helps me get on the nice list?" Santa asked if the little guy was already on the naughty list. He replied, "Oh, ya, that's for sure." Santa told the boy that he still had 3 weeks until Christmas Eve to be extra special good in everything he did and that he could probably move to the nice list. The boy nodded and ran off. His older sister and mom were across the recreation center. Santa went back to the line that had now formed. He came back, waited until the line was gone again, came back up the steps this time holding a $20 bill and blurted out, "I really thinks I still need to do this too!"

Two brothers, one 6 and one 7, came up to Santa all out of breath and yelled out, almost in unison, "So how much bad stuffs in the year counts on if you's naughty or nice, cause I'm real close."

A 7-year-old boy at a children's center party came up, took a long look at Santa, and frantically said, "Oh, oh, you're the reals Santa Claus so I gotta goes and change my story" and ran off. He showed up about an hour later looking down at the ground. Santa remembered him and asked if he had been a good little boy all year long. The boy continued to look at the ground, shifting his weight back and forth before finally replying, "Not so much, no, not really but I can splains most of it." Santa encouraged the boy to be really good the next 2 weeks to help make up for everything that went wrong during the year. The boy, still looking down, replied, "Ya, I don't see's that happening."

Chapter 9 – Parents & Grandparents

Children coming to see Santa with their parents and/or grandparents often changes the dynamics of the visit. Kids are often more open to sharing when they are alone. Parents are often looking to learn their children's Christmas wishes and pay close attention to what's being said. In these cases, Santa has learned to repeat the wish in a louder voice so that everyone can hear. I'm often asked if Santa "promises" to fulfill Christmas wishes. I use the phrase "Santa will do his best for you" in most cases. What kids say to Santa is totally unfiltered which is part of the fun of talking to the little characters. Kids can also cause horrified looks from their parents and grandparents due to their brutal honesty! When a child starts out with the words "So," it usually means they have thought something through pretty carefully and Santa better listen carefully and be ready with an answer.

A 7-year-old boy, with his parents looking on, asks in a very loud voice, "So, is Mrs. Claus a really good cook cause my dad says my mom was absent from school the day they taught cooking?" The dad's face quickly changed expressions as he looked at his wife and said, "I don't know where he got that from, dear." The boy looked at Santa again and said, "I eats cereal a lot for dinner too." The mom walked off and the dad walked closer to Santa and said, "The boy's actually telling the truth!" Must have been an interesting ride home from the party for sure.

Another 7-year-old boy came up to Santa with his parents and said, "Since you drink milk at every house, I bet you gotta pee lots, right? The mom and dad started to get a nervous look on their faces. The boy continued, "When my Grandpa takes me to Disneyland, he's gottas pee a lot and Nana says it's cause he's old like you and his plumbing is all rusted." Now the parents had horrified looks on their faces. The boy finished, "So, you and Grandpa needs to gets those diapers for old people I saw on TV, OK?" Santa stared incredulously. "Oh, and take it easy on the milk," the boy added. Mom and dad couldn't get out of there fast enough. Santa thought it was pretty funny.

An 8-year-old boy at a military base came up to Santa with his parents proudly looking on. The boy blurted out, "Are you sure you're gonna make it to Christmas Eve cause you look really old?" The mom jumped in and said, "Oh, don't say that dear." The boy looked at her and said, "But you told me to always tell the truth." The boy looked back at Santa and said, "Daddy told me that ladies change their mind a lot. Then they get 'pause and you just can't live with them." The mom looked at her husband with a stunned face, and well, I can just imagine that there was a family "discussion" on the way home.

At a children's party, a 6-year-old boy was talking on the side with his grandparents in Spanish. He came up and the Elf introduced him as Manuel. Santa smiled and said, "Hola Manny, Feliz Navidad!" The little boy's eyes got real big, and his mouth formed an O. He looked at his grandparents, then back at Santa, then back at his grandparents. He finally shouted out, "Santa said Spanish but he's white!" His grandmother said, "Santa is white, Manny." He told Santa his Christmas wishes, had his photo taken, and walked back to his grandparents, raising his arms in the air and said, "But he's white!"

Kids Say the Darndest (64) Things to Santa Claus

A 5-year-old boy came up with his mom and she told him to "go sit on Santa's lap and tell him what you'd like for Christmas." The mom turned away just then to talk to a friend. The little guy said to Santa, "I can't cause I got so excited that I pee'd in my pants!" Santa replied that it was OK to just stand next to his chair, then for the photo and his Christmas wishes. The boy replied, "OK thanks cause I don't want to mess this up, you know?"

Angel, almost 2, came to a children's employee party with his grandparents. Santa had held him the year prior for his photo with Santa Claus. In between, the little guy had open heart surgery and made it through. When the grandparents handed Angel to Santa, they beamed and both said, "He's a true Christmas miracle!"

Francisco, age 6, came to a military base employee's party with his grandparents. His parents had passed away in a horrific car crash in which he was a passenger. He had not spoken a word in the month since the accident, and his remaining family were very concerned. Santa spoke to him in Spanish, but the little boy did not respond. He stayed on the stage and sat next to Santa for an hour and a half watching and listening to all of the other children come and go. Several times, he fell asleep resting his head against Santa's leg. At the end of the party, Francisco got up and his grandparents held his hand and walked away. Suddenly he turned to Santa and said in a loud voice, "Feliz Navidad!" Both of his grandparents broke into tears and hugged their grandson. Tears of joy for sure.

A grandmother brought her 1-month-old granddaughter to a children's center party. She was fussing a bit as she tried to pass the baby to Santa. She instructed him on how to hold the baby and still support her head at the same time. Santa listened patiently, smiled and asked "First grandchild?" The woman smiled nervously and replied, "Yes and I can see you've done this before, sorry." Santa replied, "It's OK. Mrs. Claus gave me special lessons."

A 7-year-old boy came to a military base children's party with his parents. He told Santa, very seriously, that he might have to call a family meeting and have Santa there. "My mommy and daddy decided I should have a baby brother or a sister. Ever since they keeps me awake all the time cause they're in the bedroom with the door closed and making all kinds of noises." The mom and dad smiled nervously as the little guy finished by saying, "I really do needs my sleep, you knows!"

Santa had just done a few company holiday parties and was walking to his car in a parking lot to go to his office to change clothes. A family of 6 had just pulled up and got out standing in the lot. The youngest, 5, spotted Santa and came running as well as the other kids. Mom and dad soon followed. It turns out the family was moving from San Diego to Maine several days before Christmas and would be on the road for the holidays. So, it was a great serendipitous meeting for the children. As everyone talked, the oldest girl, 8, looked at Santa very seriously and said, "Why do people shoot little kids, Santa?" The horrific shooting at Sandy Hook Elementary School near where they were going to relocate had just taken place 2 weeks before. Mom and dad had very worried looks on their faces. Santa knelt down on one knee to talk to the kids. He said, "All of you are really good people, right, you 4 and your mommy and daddy?" The kids all shook their heads up and down. Santa continued, "As much as there's so many good people just like you, there's also some bad people in the world too." The kids were listening intently as were the parents. He went on, "So you have to all be extra special good to make up for the bad people. Can you promise Santa you'll do that?" Everyone nodded their heads. Santa had some candy canes and gifts in his car for another party so he got them and gave them to the kids. As the kids were unwrapping their gifts, mom and dad came up and thanked Santa. Dad said, "She's been so very quiet ever since the shooting and we were beginning to worry that it had a profound impact on her. We were concerned about this long drive and heading to the same region where it took place."

Everybody was smiling and laughing as Santa walked away to his vehicle again. Just as Santa got to his vehicle, the little boy shouted, "Wow daddy, look, Santa has an Explorer too!"

Chapter 10 – It Could Only Happen to Santa

Most of this book is about the children and their families' encounters with Santa Claus. However, in a quarter century, Santa has gone through some very "interesting" experiences, situations, and challenges himself. Working full time and being Santa provides for a very busy December to say the least. Juggling everything has been a real project some years. It has been a labor of love for sure and very fulfilling as a human being. I can't think of too many other volunteer projects that would be as meaningful. I trust that the real jolly Old Saint Nick would be proud!

Santa rarely double books himself and never, ever wears his suit in the car, but another volunteer Santa had a slight stroke, and I agreed to fill in for him the same night as my children's event. I only had a half hour between appearances, and he was an hour away. So I left the first event, stayed in the Santa suit (fortunately it was now dark), and started to drive to the next event. Being in a real hurry, I made a rolling stop at a stop sign before getting on the freeway. Of course, I got pulled over by a squad car. The officer came to the driver's side window. He looked in and exclaimed, "Oh, Jesus." I replied, "No, just Santa Claus!" He didn't look amused. After giving him my license, insurance, and registration, he said, "How am I going to explain to my four kids at breakfast tomorrow morning that I ticketed Santa Claus?" So, he let me go with a warning. I pulled back into traffic, and his lights went on again with a siren sound. I pulled over and he came back to the driver's window. He said, "Can you come with me to the front of the squad car, because I had to call in the stop and I need to close it out. This way the dash cam will record it plus no one back at the station is going to believe this!" We did, then he asked if he could take a few selfies for his kids. I said, "You know the reason I did the rolling stop was because I'm really in a hurry. I may need an escort if this takes any longer." He looked at me, all 6'2" of him and replied, "Don't push it, Santa."

For the past few years, Santa has been using a white ointment on his eye brows. After a night of appearances, Santa stopped at a local grocery store in his regular civilian clothes to get some dinner. Santa was having trouble (imagine that) on the store's self-serve checkout machine. The store attendant came over, curiously looked at me several times, fixed the problem, and started to walk away.

She turned back around, stared again and finally said, "You do know that your eyebrows are frosted right?"

Sometimes things are just meant to be. Santa was set to travel to a major fire area to make appearances at temporary housing centers and shelters. I had done it several times before, and it was much needed and meaningful work. Two nights before the Christmas Eve day appearances, the local Santa came down with a bad virus and would be unable to make the rounds. I got the call to see if I could somehow get down there in time, but all of the possible flight routes were sold out in both directions. I talked with the other Santa, who I discovered served in the military. In talking to him, it turned out that his base leader had been the guest speaker at a traveling Vietnam Wall event that I had organized 8 years earlier. He was amazed at the serendipitous timing and the fact that we knew each other. He contacted another base leader nearby about possible transport to and from the Santa appearances. Like a Christmas miracle, it all came together, and the Coordinator of the flights turned out to be my Head Elf at a military base where I had done Santa appearances for many years. What are the chances of that happening, let alone everything else? I showed up at 0600 on Christmas Eve day to fly to the fire area. My duffle bag of 2 Santa suits caused quite a bit of commotion at the base entry gate to say the least. I was also asked to leave my cell phone in my car as I was not technically on the flight. A flight officer stopped by during the flight and asked me "how you're enjoying the flight you're not on." I told him that if I had been on the flight, it would have been a great flight." After arriving, I was picked up outside the base and transported to a total of 11 stops before flying home again on a flight that I wasn't really on. I got in my car at the base and wrote down dozens of stories and then drove home thinking about how this could only happen to Santa Claus. I inquired about putting this in the book and was told that as long as I didn't use any staff names, actual base names or too much specific information, it "may" be ok. That was enough for me to share it with you!

A close, lifelong friend of Santa annually invites him to both Thanksgiving and Christmas at her home to share the Holidays with friends. Santa rarely is able to attend due to his real job. One year it turned out Santa would be able to leave work a bit early and show up conveniently at dessert time. He was very excited and texted his host that he would be on his way soon for the hour drive plus would come dressed as Santa! His host was thrilled and said it would be a great surprise and lots of fun for everyone gathered. As Santa got to the final 2 blocks before arriving at his host's home, he realized that he didn't have a plan for changing into the Santa suit. Fortunately, it was now dark. Now a block away from his destination, Santa saw that on one side of the street was an apartment complex with a high brick wall and on the other side of the street was a high brick wall with houses behind it. Santa pulled up to the side of the street across from the apartment complex. He got out, opened up the passenger front door and back door of his Explorer in order to change clothes between them. It takes roughly 20-30 minutes to "suit up" as us Santa calls it. Now half-dressed and half-undressed, Santa got that panicked feeling which comes over all of us one time or another. What if someone in the apartment complex looked out their window? What if someone walking their pet dog came on the sidewalk behind Santa? What if a car came down the street or worse, a squad car? Adding to the panic, Santa was struggling to pull on his large black boots without anything to steady himself on. Sure enough, Santa fell full force backwards and banged the back of his head on the concrete sidewalk. Laying there half-dressed, Santa could only wonder if he would be found this way if he passed out. Those who know this Santa know that he can be a "tad" accident prone, so none of this was a big surprise. Santa was finally able to stand up, steady himself, finish dressing, and arrived at his hosts home as if nothing ever happened. It was a fun night for all in attendance taking photos and toasting. Later Santa went into the bathroom and changed into his civilian clothes and returned to the party as if he had just arrived. Only the Host knew for sure who Santa was!

There's just no way for Santa Claus to hide in public. One year, Santa did several parties for the Sales' department staff. Returning to the Casino, Santa tried to sneak into the employee hallway to change clothes. Too late. Two families of four and six spotted him waiting to go into the casino buffet. When you're Santa, you just can't wave people off, especially children. So, Santa went over and visited with the families. By now the Surveillance staff had spotted him. Disguises, masks, and anything covering the face are not allowed. The buffet was next to the Steak House and soon Santa also had to go into that restaurant to visit with several families that had heard the commotion and Ho-Ho-Ho's. What had started out as a quick retreat into an employee hallway had turned into a half hour public appearance, all against policy. In the Steak House, two security officers had arrived and told Santa he needed to take off his beard, wig, and glasses. Santa announced to the kids that the officers were going to escort him back to his sleigh. Once back safely in the employee hallway, the two officers and Santa had a good, hearty laugh about the whole thing.

Yes Virginia, there really is a Santa Claus. In this case, however, it applies to adults as well. Imagine being in your mid-thirties and never knowing about Santa. That very man came to an employee housing holiday party full of jubilance and anticipation. Ethiopia was his home, and he had only been in the U.S. for a year. He'd only heard stories about Santa Claus since his arrival in the states. He patiently waited in line, smiling bright and wide, until it was his turn to meet the legend. He told

Santa he had arranged a gathering at his parent's home in Ethiopia for a live Facetime with Santa. 28 people had gathered at his childhood home for this special occasion. They were all in a festive mood, celebrating their relatives first-ever time meeting Santa and joining in this Western tradition. He sat cross-legged directly in front of Santa and as the man and Santa waved into the cell phone, his entire family cheered. When it was over, he had teared up and just quietly said, "Thank you for that." The world proved to be both big and small that day.

Dedications & Special Thank You's

I am appreciative, humbled, and eternally grateful to be able to share this collection of stories with children and former children of all ages. The opportunities given to me to be part of the holiday season each year is something I will forever treasure. The event organizers, Mrs. Claus, Elves, staff members of numerous organizations, servicemen and women, first responders, medical professionals, parents, grandparents, and children made my holiday season the best part of every year. Not having children of my own, I've learned how to be Santa Claus to children by observing wonderful role model parents, grandparents, and relatives' examples through the years. My dedications and thank you's are just my small way of saying, "THANKS!"

For the book itself:

Keith James Kennedy aka Keith JK – My editor, a 3-time published author, but more importantly my nephew. His advice, dedication to the project, and determination to help make it happen was awesome.

Jackie Brett – My lifetime special friend, also a published author, who provided inspiration, support, and a world of ideas. She is a longtime Las Vegas Advertising & Publicity professional who continues to write several major columns from Las Vegas.

Peggy Bendel – Author and world class destination marketing, crisis communications & media training guru & President of Bendel Communications International. She wrote a comment to me on Facebook in 2013 after I posted some of my very first Santa stories: "There's a book here, Don!" She provided me with support, ideas, and encouragement. Peggy & I worked together for the Pueblo of Acoma Sky City when it opened its wonderful Cultural Center & Museum in New Mexico.

Nikki & JT Woods – Longtime special friends who gave me a treasured family book by fellow Santa, Bob Kreutzer, titled "It Could Only Happen to Santa Claus," which prodded me to do the same. They are amazing parents as well.

Dr. Keller Coker – Dean of the New School for Jazz & Contemporary Music in New York City, longtime friend, co-creator of memorable special events, concerts, and promotions. He too many times said, "DK, you need to write a book!"

Larry Lambert – Casino Host, longtime friend, and co-worker. My sounding board, inspiration, and "don't ever give up" associate. He encouraged me to write this book many times.

To the best Santa ever: Kenny Bob Davis – My lifetime friend and mentor.

For being an amazing Mrs. Claus: Marlena Kesler and Teresa Lusk

For being thought of & invited to be their Santa: Children's Centers, Boys & Girls Clubs, hospitals, churches, military bases, casinos, recreation centers, schools, charitable organizations, shelters, and other sites in Nevada, California, Louisiana, Illinois, Indiana, Oklahoma, New Mexico, and Oregon.

To Casino General Managers/CEO's & Vice Presidents who understood the importance of giving back to the employees and community by hosting holiday children's events: Marvis Aragon, Joseph "JQ" Quiroli, Stuart Richey, Shana Tucker, Jim Kikumoto, Gregg Shutiva, and James Ervin.

To several hundred Elves over the years and in particular Lois "Joei" Wood, Ron Sakaniwa, Johnathan "JT" Smith, Lloyd Tortilita, Niki-Gratson Middleton, Robin Johnson, Martin Deaver, James Boggs, Karina Durante, Larry Elliott, John Simonton, Joseph Fry, and Bill Montague.

For the wonderful role models of what parents, grandparents, and relatives are supposed to be when dealing with children. Thanks for inviting me into your families' lives so I could observe and grow in my understanding of children and how to provide a meaningful experience visiting with them as their Santa Claus. I learned the very best from the very best: Dorothy & Howard Kennedy, Judy & Jim Marshall, Maureen Kennedy-Harlan & Scott Harlan, James Frederick Kennedy, Jeanne & Steve Foltz, Eileen Marie, Shana & Michael Tucker, Nancy Arca, Dawn Bredimus, Christine & Tom Tuchschmidt, Christie & Mike Pierce,

Shirley & Pat Dunne, Rene Guim, Julie
& Joe Gutierrez – whose grandson
Angel is mentioned in the
Parents/Grandparents section, Andrew
Reno, Deb & Jimmy McClelland, Maria
Esther, Darrus Chafee, Denise & Jack
Tatum, Kathy Imboden, In Choi, Paul
Ziegler, Mariana & Runi Tafeaga, Mary
Lattin, Cynthia & Don Hughes, Tammy
Tinfo & Preston Lum, Juanita Johnson,
Jo Porter, Diane & Jim Kusz, Dana &
Gary Yelverton, Pamela & Brian
Craveiro, Juli-Chavez Slocum &
Stephen Slocum, Janelle Kennedy,
Travis Lewis, Colleen & Steve
Mahoney, Debbie Whitmer Kennedy,
Nikki & JT Woods, Crystal & Ricky
Wood, Robin & Kelly Mays, Jami &
Chris Zesiger, Grace Morrison,
Marionette Kaahue Miriam Del Toro &
Norques, Pat & Roger Robertson,
Patricia & Robert Everhart, Becky &
Joe Hernandez, Tara & Aaron Will,
Rhonda & Larry Lambert, Mary & Tom
Davis, Amanda Mock & David
Schachter, Niki Gratson-Middleton &

David Middleton, Priscilla & Soli
Gonzalez, Bernadette & Richard
Mirabal, Mary Kate Nash, CJ & Gregg
Shutiva, Marvis Aragon, Lissa & Joel
Leong, Flo & Ken Leong, Didi & Paul Ah
Yo, Katrina Kennedy-Albrandt & James
Albrandt, Michele Sobczyk, Dan
Randall, Rosa Malespin, Matthew
Mingrone, Anne & Victor Reyes,
Shannon & Steve Chrisman (Steve
"Cheese" also wrote a book & said, "If
I can, you can!"), Anne & Rod
Sherman, Darcy & Clay Marshall,
Delores & Ed Ben, Eldaa & Bill Daily,
Sharon & Jim Gillen, Hope-McCarty
Romero, Mother Teresa Robb
Simmons, The Whitmers: Scott, Brent,
Heather & families, Mary & Eddie
Lattin, Joan & Manny Loya, Dawn &
Stuart Richey, The Schermer ladies:
Karen, Sharen, Elaine & families, Sallie
Ann Hollingsworth, Maria & Paul
Vasquez, Henry "HG" Gomez, Lori &
Kris Rogers, Janet & Matt Lepien,
Karen & Ed Wickman, Linda & John
Kelly, Jackie Hobson, Maria & Jose

Torres, Ana & Angel Soriano, Iris
Kennedy, Theresa & David Reisenauer,
Kim & Steve Gravois, Shayna & Wilford
Holt, Gayle & John Herbert, Pam
Bouillon, Mike & Christopher Davis,
Deborah Dean Davis, The Leong guys:
Ryan, Kalae & families, Sue & Harold
Buchanan, The Lum guys: Eric,
Spencer & Chase, Talia Rice, Bonnie &
Wayne Mackey, Carolyn Hook & Bud,
Ana & Matthew Mingrone, Cookie,
Heather & Rob Jozwiak, Linda & Roger
Sprague, Bonnie & Mike Holden,
Rachel & Phil Robertson, Katie & Logan
Timberlake, The Mays guys: Waylon,
Dayton, Eric & families, Debbie Nessler
Zaffiro, & Peggi Sanders.

If I forgot anyone, blame it on
Rudolph!

DON KENNEDY

BIO

Don Kennedy is a longtime resident of Las Vegas, Nevada. He's a first-time author, or as the infamous W.C. Fields called it, a "scrivener."

Born and raised in Wisconsin, Kennedy is a graduate of Concordia College. He began writing as the editor of his high school newspaper and sports reporter for the local city newspaper.

He was a radio and TV broadcaster as well as a print editor/publisher for more than a decade. Kennedy was a city editor and sports editor for the Henderson Home News and Boulder City News, a reporter for the Pahrump Valley Times, an editor of Vegarama, Las Vegas Top Spots and Las Vegas Pizazz magazine, a publisher/editor of Going Places/Southwest Traveler magazine, and a feature writer for Valley Electric's Ruralite magazine. He was also a radio personality on KVOV and KREL radio stations while simultaneously hosting a syndicated travel radio program, "Going Places," on the local NBC Talk Radio station. He provided voice-overs and commercial broadcasting for several TV stations.

For the past 35 years, Kennedy has been a casino marketing executive with titles of manager, director, vice president, corporate vice president, AGM, and CMO in seven states: Nevada, California, Oregon, New Mexico, Louisiana, Indiana and Oklahoma. He has served as a judge for the prestigious Romero Awards and been a guest speaker/lecturer at numerous seminars, conferences, conventions and several universities. He has worked the past decade as Player Development Manager at Primm Valley Casino & Resorts, part of Affinity Gaming. A Roast/Toast celebrating his career was held in 2015 and is available on YouTube titled "Don Kennedy Roast Primm 2015."

In his rare free time, Kennedy enjoys travel, especially where there are lakes and oceans. He has been an active member and officer of the NFL Alumni Association for 20 years as an Associate Member. He's a proud uncle to two nieces, a nephew, grandniece and grandnephew, and has an older brother.

Kennedy's nickname is "The Phantom," given to him by mentor and renowned casino marketing guru, John Romero, because no one could keep track of him with his casino hospitality career constantly moving him around the country. Where he would land, nobody knew.

His passion, every December for the past 25 years, has been serving as a volunteer Santa Claus for all those who needed to be seen, heard, and given a little Christmas spirit.

What are Some of the "Darndest Things" your Kids have Said to Santa Claus?

_____

_____

_____

_____

_____

_____

_____

_____

_____

_____

_____

_____

_____

_____

_____

_____

_____

_____

_____

_____

_____

_____

_____

_____

_____

_____

_____

_____

_____

_____

_____

Kids Say the Darndest (94) Things to Santa Claus

_____

_____

_____

_____

_____

_____

_____

_____

_____

_____

_____

_____

_____

_____

_____

_____

_____

_____

_____

Kids Say the Darndest (95) Things to Santa Claus

_____

_____

_____

_____

_____

_____

_____

_____

_____

_____

_____

_____

_____

_____

_____

_____

_____

_____

Kids Say the Darndest (96) Things to Santa Claus

_____

_____

_____

_____

_____

_____

_____

_____

_____

_____

_____

_____

_____

_____

_____

_____

_____

Kids Say the Darndest (97) Things to Santa Claus

_____

_____

_____

_____

_____

_____

_____

_____

_____

_____

_____

_____

_____

_____

_____

_____

_____

Kids Say the Darndest (98) Things to Santa Claus

_____

_____

_____

_____

_____

_____

_____

_____

_____

_____

_____

_____

_____

_____

_____

_____

_____

_____

Kids Say the Darndest (99) Things to Santa Claus